NOW YOU CAN READ ABOUT...

WHALES and SHARKS

TEXT BY MARY HOFFMAN

ILLUSTRATED BY COLIN NEWMAN

BRIMAX BOOKS • NEWMARKET • ENGLAND

The biggest animals in the world
are whales. They live in the sea.
Whales are mammals not fishes.
This means they are warm-blooded.
Dolphins and porpoises belong to
the same family as whales. They
are sea-mammals too. A group of
sea-mammals is called a "school".

Sharks live in the sea. They are fishes. They are cold-blooded. Look at this shark. It is as long as the boat.

Most sharks have rows of sharp teeth. Sharks are very fast swimmers.

Some whales have teeth. Some whales have tusks too. The narwhal is a white whale. It has one tusk.

The beluga is also a white whale. White whales live in seas near the North Pole.

Some whales do
not have teeth.
They have bony
plates in their
jaws called
"baleen".
They take a huge gulp of
sea-water. Then they slowly spit
the water out, trapping the food
behind the baleen.

Some baleen whales feed on tiny creatures called plankton. Others eat fish.

The blue whale is the biggest living animal. It weighs the same as 33 elephants.

Look at this
sperm whale.
It is diving deep
to catch squid.

Whales spend most of their life
under water. Like you, they use
their lungs to breathe. After
a dive they blow air and water
out of a hole in their heads.

Whale babies grow for over a year inside their mother. One baby is born at a time. The calf drinks its mother's milk under water.

Right whales have their calves in the warm sea near Argentina. The babies stay with their mother for over a year.

Whale calves can swim when they are a few hours old. They soon learn to play round their mothers in the water. The babies make their flippers and tails strong by flapping them. When they are six months old they swim out to deeper water to catch food.

Whales have thick layers of fat to keep their blood warm. This kind of fat is called "blubber". People have hunted whales for over a thousand years. They use the blubber to make oil.

There are not many whales left now. They are hunted today for meat and for blubber. Would you like to eat whale meat? Some countries have laws to stop the killing of whales.

Dolphins and porpoises are warm-blooded, like whales. Dolphins are very clever. Look at this dolphin. If they are left in the sea, dolphins live for fifty years.

The black and
white killer whale
is a dolphin
really. It kills
fish and penguins.
It does not kill
people!

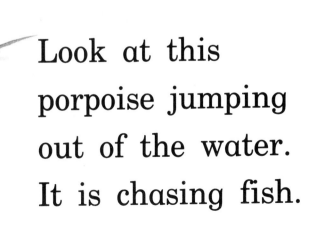

Look at this
porpoise jumping
out of the water.
It is chasing fish.

We think sharks are dangerous. But most kinds of shark are harmless to people. The basking shark has no teeth. It floats on the water eating plankton and small fish.

The whale shark also eats plankton and small fish. It is the biggest kind there is. It can be longer than a sailing ship.

The small black fish is a dwarf shark. It is the smallest shark. The other fish is a mackerel.

This shark is dangerous! It is the great white shark. It attacks people or any creature it meets.

This hammerhead shark also attacks people. Can you see why it is called "hammerhead"?

Can you see the wobbegong hiding on the sea bottom? This fish is also called the carpet shark. It is dangerous because it is hard to see. A swimmer might get a nasty bite on the foot. Wobbegongs live near the coast of Australia.

Like other fish, some sharks lay eggs. Other sharks give birth to live babies. The hammerhead has about 30 babies at once. The babies grow inside their mother for about two years. As soon as they are born the baby sharks start hunting for food.

All sharks are very fast swimmers. They have long slim bodies. This helps them to move easily through the water. They have a good sense of smell and swim fast towards the smell of blood. The shark is a fast and fierce hunter.

Now you have read about large sea creatures. Do you know what these are called?